Keys to Effective Evangelism

Keys to Effective Evangelism

by
John MacArthur, Jr.

MOODY PRESS
CHICAGO

All Scripture quotations, unless noted otherwise, are from the *New Scofield
Reference Bible*, King James Version. Copyright © 1967 by Oxford Univer-
sity Press, Inc. Reprinted by permission.

Library of Congress Cataloging in Publication Data

MacArthur, John, 1939-
    Keys to effective evangelism.

    (John MacArthur's Bible studies)
    Includes indexes.
    1. Bible.   N.T.   Acts V, 12 - VI, 7—Criticism,
interpretation, etc.   2. Evangelistic work—Biblical
teaching.   I. Title.   II. Series: MacArthur, John,
1939-   .   Bible studies.
BS2625.2.M266   1988   269'.2   88-7199
ISBN 0-8024-5361-9

1 2 3 4 5 6 Printing/LC/Year 93 92 91 90 89 88

Printed in the United States of America

Contents

These Bible studies are taken from messages delivered by Pastor-Teacher John MacArthur, Jr., at Grace Community Church in Panorama City, California. The recorded messages themselves may be purchased as a series or individually. Please request the current price list by writing to:

WORD OF GRACE COMMUNICATIONS
P.O. Box 4000
Panorama City, CA 91412

Or call the following toll-free number:
1-800-55-GRACE

1

The Early Church Pattern for Evangelism
—Part 1

Outline

Introduction
A. An Analysis of the Church's Growth
    1. Rapid growth
    2. Real growth
    3. Regular growth
B. The Annals of the Church's Growth

Lesson
I. Purity (vv. 12*b*-14)
    A. A Mandate for Purity
        1. The proof
            a) Stated
            b) Illustrated
        2. The process
            a) Matthew 18:15
            b) Matthew 18:16
            c) Matthew 18:17*a*
            d) Matthew 18:17*b*
        3. The pattern
    B. A Model of Purity
        1. A record of the church's purity (v. 12*b*)
        2. The results of the church's purity (vv. 13-14)
            a) Stated negatively (v. 13*a*)
            b) Stated positively (v. 13*b*-14)

II. Power (vv. 12a, 15-16)
   A. Seen Through Signs and Wonders (v. 12a)
   B. Seen Through Healings (vv. 15-16)

Conclusion

Introduction

In Acts 5:12-42 Luke reveals the early church's pattern of evangelism.

   A. An Analysis of the Church's Growth

      1. Rapid growth

         From its inception the church grew rapidly. Acts 2:41 says that on the Day of Pentecost "there were added unto them about three thousand souls." Acts 2:47 says, "The Lord added to the church daily such as should be saved." In Acts 4:4 we discover that "the number of the men [Gk., *anēr*, "adult male"] was about five thousand." Acts 5:14 says, "Believers were the more added to the Lord, multitudes both of men and women." In Acts 6:7 Luke records that "the number of the disciples multiplied in Jerusalem greatly." Acts 8:6 notes that in response to Philip's ministry "the people with one accord gave heed." Acts 9:31 says, "Then had the churches rest throughout all Judaea and Galilee and Samaria, and were edified; and walking in the fear of the Lord, and in the comfort of the Holy Spirit, were multiplied." In Acts 11:21 Luke says that "a great number believed," and in verse 24 he reiterates that "many people were added unto the Lord." The church was growing so quickly that within weeks thousands had joined. Believers were actively evangelizing; the church was reaching the world.

      2. Real growth

         That tremendous growth continued even though being a Christian at that time was difficult. The price was high, the demands were extreme, and total commitment was

8

essential. But after having counted the cost, many still came to Christ. There's nothing wrong with tremendous growth if it's the result of evangelism—that's the only kind of growth that is real. Those Christians wanted to win others to Jesus Christ, and through the empowerment of the Holy Spirit they were able to. Because their only motive was God's glory, the Holy Spirit magnified their work. Later in Acts when Paul and Barnabas reported the conversion of Gentiles, "they caused great joy unto all the brethren" (15:3). There's nothing more exciting to believers than being used by God to draw others to Himself.

3. Regular growth

Today some suggest that when a church reaches a certain number of people it should stop reaching out. The early church in Jerusalem had three thousand the first day—and had just begun! It's tragic for a church to become satisfied with its growth. Regardless of how many believers there are, there need to be more. Those who know Christ can't be content merely to attend their churches, feast on the Word, and excuse themselves from reaching others, thinking, *There are so many here already.* Because evangelism is our mission, everything we learn should make us more effective in winning others to Christ.

B. The Annals of the Church's Growth

In Acts 1 we see the Lord equipping the future church, as it still remained in the womb of God's promise. Then in chapter 2 the church is born. Immediately it began to grow and was nurtured in "the apostles' doctrine and fellowship, and in breaking of bread, and in prayers" (2:42). Naturally with growth came opposition, and its infant muscles were tested. But it became stronger as a result. The church's task was simple: to reach the world. And it was totally committed to it. In chapter 4 they pray, "Lord, behold their threatenings; and grant unto thy servants, that with all boldness they may speak thy word, by stretching forth thine hand to heal; and that signs and wonders may be done by the name of thy holy child, Jesus. And when they had prayed, the place was shaken where they were

9

assembled together; and they were all filled with the Holy Spirit, and they spoke the word of God with boldness" (vv. 29-31). These members of the early church were committed to evangelism.

They were committed not only to evangelism, but also to each other. Acts 4:32-37 stresses that there was unity and sharing. That text describes two essentials for effective evangelism: individuals proclaiming the Word and a collective unity. Jesus emphasized the importance of unity when He prayed that His followers might be one so that the world would believe that the Father sent the Son (John 17:21). In John 13:35 He tells His disciples, "By this shall all men know that ye are my disciples, if ye have love one to another." Their evangelism flowed naturally from personal communication and collective unity. But at that point Satan struck. In chapter 5 a great sin that threatened to be a blight on the church surfaces. Ananias and Sapphira lied to the Holy Spirit in an effort to be considered spiritual. God disciplined them before the whole church by taking their lives, illustrating the severity of sin in the church. Thus God immediately cut out the cancer that had crept into the church. When we get to verse 12, the church is pure again, and evangelism is ready to flourish.

Lesson

Acts 5:12-42 highlights five progressive features that are keys to effective evangelism.

I. PURITY (vv. 12b-14)

"They were all with one accord in Solomon's porch. And of the rest dared no man join himself to them; but the people magnified them. And believers were the more added to the Lord, multitudes both of men and women."

A. A Mandate for Purity

1. The proof

10

a) Stated

In Acts 5:1-11 God disciplines Ananias and Sapphira because the church must be pure to make an impression on the world. Nineteenth-century Scottish minister Robert Murray McCheyne said, "It is not great talents God blesses so much as great likeness to Jesus. A holy minister is an awful weapon in the hand of God" (*Memoirs of McCheyne*, Andrew A. Bonar, ed. [Chicago: Moody, 1947], p. 95). To reach the world the church must be pure. I believe God still purifies the church as He does in Acts 5.

Hebrews 12:6 says, "Whom the Lord loveth he chasteneth, and scourgeth every son whom he receiveth." First Corinthians 11:30 reveals that God took the lives of some Corinthian believers because they had abused the Lord's Table. First John 5:16 refers to "a sin unto death." Although God still disciplines directly, today He has primarily committed discipline within the church to its leaders and members. We are responsible to discipline not only our own lives but also the lives of those around us. After examining our own hearts, we must be alert for sin in the church. Ephesians 5:11 says, "Have no fellowship with the unfruitful works of darkness but, rather, reprove them." First Timothy 5:20 says, "Them that sin rebuke before all, that others also may fear." In 1 Timothy 1:20 Paul mentions Hymenaeus and Alexander by name, saying they were "delivered unto Satan, that they [might] learn not to blaspheme." In Titus 1:13 Paul exhorts Titus to rebuke unruly believers "sharply, that they may be sound in the faith." In Luke 17:3 Jesus says, "If thy brother trespass against thee, rebuke him." The church must examine sin within itself because purity is basic to evangelism.

b) Illustrated

First Corinthians 5:1-6 says, "It is reported commonly that there is fornication [sexual sin] among you, and such fornication as is not so much as named among the Gentiles [heathen], that one should have his father's wife. And ye are puffed up [proud of your sin], and have not rather mourned, that he that hath done this deed might be taken away from among you. For I verily, as absent in body but present in spirit, have judged already, as though I were present, concerning him that hath done this deed, in the name of our Lord Jesus Christ, when ye are gathered together, and my spirit, with the power of our Lord Jesus Christ, to deliver such an one unto Satan [to put him out of the church] for the destruction of the flesh, that the spirit may be saved in the day of the Lord Jesus. . . . Know ye not that a little leaven leaveneth the whole lump?" The church must deal with sin.

2. The process

   In Matthew 18 Christ presents a clear process for dealing with sin in the church.

   a) Matthew 18:15—"If thy brother shall trespass against thee, go and tell him his fault between thee and him alone; if he shall hear thee, thou hast gained thy brother." It's amazing how many Christians refuse to go to the one who has done wrong. Instead they create a circle of gossip. It is biblical to approach the person himself first.

   b) Matthew 18:16—"But if he will not hear thee, then take with thee one or two more, that in the mouth of two or three witnesses every word may be established." Your responsibility doesn't end once you have gone to a sinning brother privately and he has refused to listen. Take two or three others with you and lovingly confront him with his sin again.

   c) Matthew 18:17*a*—"If he shall neglect to hear them, tell it unto the church." This is what you do if he refuses to listen to all of you.

   d) Matthew 18:17*b*—"If he neglect to hear the church, let him be unto thee as an heathen man and a tax collector." That doesn't mean he loses his salvation; it

12

means he should be put outside the fellowship because he will harm it by bringing in his sin. The church is committing the sinning brother to God's discipline. Practicing church discipline can raise some difficult problems. But the early church never sidestepped difficult issues. Those believers understood what was at stake: not the feelings of a sinning brother, but a pure church from which to communicate the gospel to the world. It's a question of priorities.

3. The pattern

God Himself was the first to practice church discipline to show how critical purity is. Commentator Harry Ironside said, "If the Spirit of God were working in that way today, what a lot of work there would be for the undertakers!" (*Lectures on the Book of Acts* [N.J.: Loizeaux, 1975], p. 132). The sin of Ananias and Sapphira was a gash in the body of the infant church; a splash of filth on the white raiment of God's chosen. In 1 Peter 4:17 Peter says, "Judgment must begin at the house of God."

B. A Model of Purity

Acts 5:12b-14 is a large parenthetical comment that discusses the purity of the early church in Jerusalem.

1. A record of the church's purity (v. 12b)

"They were all with one accord in Solomon's porch."

The sin within the church had been rooted out, and all were at one accord—the church was pure again. That doesn't mean all the members were sinlessly perfect. It means they were being honest with God and confessing their sin, not hiding it deceitfully as were Ananias and Sapphira. Luke said they were all in "Solomon's porch," which was one of the elevated sides of the great court of the Temple. Peter and John healed a man there, and then Peter preached there (3:17-26). Thus Solomon's Porch had apparently become a customary place for Christians to assemble daily for the times of prayer in the Temple. It was a perfect spot, because at the times of prayer masses of people crowded into the courtyard. Those Christians who were elevated slightly on Solomon's Porch would be able to draw the attention and interest of everyone there.

2. The results of the church's purity (vv. 13-14)

   a) Stated negatively (v. 13*a*)

   "Of the rest dared no man join himself to them."

   No one else dared to join the Christians who had gathered in Solomon's Porch. Usually when something is new, exciting, and fast-growing, people are eager to jump on the bandwagon. But not in this case. Verse 5 says, "Ananias . . . fell down, and died; and great fear came on all them that heard these things." Verses 10-11 add, "Then fell [Sapphira] down immediately at his feet, and died. . . . And great fear came upon all the church, and upon as many as heard these things." People weren't anxious to join that movement because it was dangerous. Only those who were totally committed to Jesus Christ became part of the church. It was too risky for those who weren't. Unless they are totally committed, people naturally avoid any relationship where their sin will be confronted. Only those whom God was adding became part of the church. Discipline in the church is important because it makes our evangelism pure and protects us from the infiltration of the world.

Total Commitment: Jesus' Requirement for Church Membership

Today's churches are filled with sinning saints. Because there's no price to belonging, people who don't belong constantly infiltrate the church. There's nothing to fear, and church membership can be advantageous to them. The problem is that most churches don't require any deep commitment of their members. Consequently unbelievers, hypocrites, and people with shallow commitments infiltrate the church and obstruct the purity that should characterize it. Membership in the church of Jesus Christ demands a total life com-

14

mitment. God's standard is perfection, even beyond what we can experience or understand. When anyone can belong and become involved, the church becomes impure and obscures the truth. I am not saying we shouldn't welcome those who don't know Jesus Christ—we welcome them wholeheartedly with His love because we want them to come to Christ. But when they come to unite with His church, we must stress God's standards for admission. By that we're not trying to keep them out, but we are telling them God's requirements: total commitment to Jesus Christ.

b) Stated positively (v. 13*b*-14)

> "But the people magnified them. And believers were the more added to the Lord, multitudes both of men and women."

> Only believers were added to the church. That is the way it is supposed to be. We need purity that is motivated not by legalism but by a love for God, who desires to keep His church pure. Christianity is plagued today by a multitude of unsaved church members, who can hide in the church because it seldom confronts sin and sometimes even allows membership to anyone who asks. A frequent excuse for not disciplining is the fear of offending. But that's like saying, "I don't want to tell my lungs that they have cancer because they might be offended."

The Church's Check System

When I talk about the responsibility of the church, I'm not talking about the church on the corner or a particular denomination but about the church that includes every Christian. Each believer has the responsibility to maintain personal purity and to help fellow believers do the same. We do that by our example and rebuking them of sin we are aware of. Knowing that other believers are lovingly watching our lives helps us to be pure. It's a check system. If you know something in your life is wrong, make it right. If you know of sin in the life of a brother, go to him privately and admonish him in love. If the church is pure, our evangelism will also be pure.

Some argue that such teaching will keep unbelievers from attending church. It may be that those people fear they themselves will be discovered. However, real evangelism begins with a pure church. When the church is pure, *God* adds genuine believers to it. If the price of membership is high—as it ought to be—the church will be composed of legitimate members. Although our love extends to everyone because of Jesus' death for them, people must understand the cost of belonging and weigh it carefully. Our churches must not allow unbelievers to hide in the church as members. Because we love them, we should want them to truly know Jesus Christ.

Jesus' High Standard for Belonging to Him

Luke 9:57-58 says, "It came to pass that, as they went on the way, a certain man said unto [Jesus], Lord, I will follow thee wherever thou goest. And Jesus said unto him, Foxes have holes, and birds of the air have nests, but the Son of man hath not where to lay his head." Somewhere between verse 58 and 59 that man leaves and never returns. Verse 59 says, "He said unto another, Follow me. But he said, Lord, permit me first to go and bury my father." This man's father was probably still living. Perhaps he wanted to wait until his father died and he had received his inheritance before following Christ. The Lord responded, "Let the dead [those who are spiritually dead] bury their dead [those who are physically dead]; but go thou and preach the kingdom of God" (v. 60). Apparently that man also left. Verses 61-62 continue, "Another also said, Lord, I will follow thee; but let me first go bid them farewell, who are at home at my house. And Jesus said unto him, No man, having put his hand to the plow, and looking back, is fit for the kingdom of God." Christ demands total commitment.

In Matthew 10:32-39 Jesus says, "Whosoever, therefore, shall confess me before men, him will I confess also before my Father, who is in heaven. But whosoever shall deny me before men, him will I also deny before my Father, who is in heaven. Think not that I am come to send peace on earth; I am come not to send peace, but a sword. For I am come to set a man at variance against his father, and the daughter against her mother, and the daughter-in-law against her mother-in-law. And a man's foes shall be they of his

16

own household. He that loveth father or mother more than me, is not worthy of me; and he that loveth son or daughter more than me, is not worthy of me. And he that taketh not his cross and followeth after me, is not worthy of me. He that findeth his life shall lose it; and he that loseth his life for my sake shall find it." He seeks people who will lose everything and follow Him.

Some may believe that kind of commitment produces a weighty and slavish life. Others may wonder why anyone would want to become a Christian. In Matthew 11:28-30 Christ balances the demand for total commitment by saying, "Come unto me, all ye that labor and are heavy laden, and I will give you rest. Take my yoke upon you, and learn of me; for I am meek and lowly in heart, and ye shall find rest unto your souls. For my yoke is easy, and my burden is light." The Lord demands total commitment, but once we are willing to make it, He shoulders the rest of our burden. Knowing Jesus Christ is truly a great joy.

Notice that the last part of verse 14 speaks of "multitudes both of men and women." The church grew so fast that they stopped counting. A pure, saved, fully committed membership is the key to real growth. Evangelism begins as we emphasize purity within our own lives and churches.

II. POWER (vv. 12a, 15-16)

A pure church will always have power, and the church in Jerusalem had it. The Sanhedrin had threatened the apostles against any public ministry (4:18). No one could speak about the resurrection. But it's impossible to hide the power of a pure church, so they were bold, and the church progressed.

A. Seen Through Signs and Wonders (v. 12a)

"And by the hands of the apostles were many signs and wonders wrought among the people."

The apostles were regularly doing miracles. The gifts of miracles, healings, tongues, and interpretations of tongues were sign gifts, which God gave to the apostles and certain Old Testament prophets to confirm the Word. After seeing

17

the miracles that the apostles did in the name of Jesus Christ, the people were open to hearing about Him. Those miracles verified the apostles' message. In fact, in 2 Corinthians 12:12 Paul calls miraculous gifts "the signs of an apostle." Hebrews 2:4 speaks of the apostles having certain miraculous gifts of the Holy Spirit, which they used to verify the validity of their message. Jesus Himself used miracles to confirm His message. He went into a town, performed miracles, and then told the people who He was.

The miracles in Acts 5 are an answer to the church's prayer in chapter 4, where they say, "Grant unto thy servants, that with all boldness they may speak thy word, by stretching forth thine hand to heal; and that signs and wonders may be done by the name of thy holy child, Jesus" (vv. 29-30). But God couldn't grant that request until the church was pure. The Greek words translated *signs* and *wonders* emphasize their purpose. "Signs" point to something, and "wonders" create an attitude of amazement. All the miracles pointed to the deity of Jesus Christ and created wonder in the minds of the people.

B. Seen Through Healings (vv. 15-16)

"Insomuch that they brought forth the sick into the streets, and laid them on beds [the valuable, soft beds of the rich] and couches [the typical beds of the poor], that at the least the shadow of Peter passing by might overshadow some of them. There came also a multitude out of the cities round about unto Jerusalem, bringing sick folks, and them who were vexed with unclean spirits; and they were healed every one."

The streets of Jerusalem were an incredible sight. Everywhere there were beds occupied by rich and poor alike, all waiting for the apostles to move through town. The inhabitants of Jerusalem actually believed that Peter's shadow could heal. Some ancient peoples believed that a man's shadow carried his influence, so parents would place their children into the shadow of great men and snatch them away from the shadow of someone they disliked. The text doesn't say that Peter's shadow healed anyone—only that the people believed so. Their actions displayed a tremendous respect for Peter. Great miracles indeed occurred.

Can We Expect Miracles Today?

Someone may ask, "If the church is pure today, will all those miracles continue?" No. The miraculous gifts have passed away because they were for the establishment of the church (cf. Heb. 2:3-4). There is no biblical promise that those miracles would continue. Some people argue that such miracles can happen today because we live in the end times. But the Holy Spirit says that at the end of this age there will be apostasy, lawlessness, departure from the faith, false religions, delusions, and doctrines of devils—no miracles. However, the Bible does say there will be signs and wonders. Second Thessalonians 2:9 says there will be "power and signs and lying wonders" propagated by Satan. Although Paul is referring to the events surrounding the Tribulation, we've already begun to see "the mystery of iniquity" at work (2 Thess. 2:7). Some "lying wonders" are happening even now under demonic influence.

The early church was a powerful church. The church today can be as well—if it is pure. The same applies to every individual believer. Reminding Timothy of the priorities for ministry, Paul said, "Keep thyself pure" (1 Tim. 5:22).

Conclusion

Second Timothy 2:19-21 says, "The foundation of God standeth sure, having this seal, The Lord knoweth them that are his; and, Let every one that nameth the name of Christ depart from iniquity. But in a great house there are not only vessels of gold and of silver, but also of wood and of earth; and some to honor, and some to dishonor. If a man, therefore, purge himself from these, he shall be a vessel unto honor, sanctified, and fit for the master's use, and prepared unto every good work." Clay, wood, silver, and gold vessels are all in the Father's house, but no one wants to be a clay pot when he could be a gold one. No one wants to be on a shelf when he could be fit for the Master's use. Keep yourself pure. As each Christian keeps himself pure and keeps his brothers and sisters in Christ accountable, the church will have the power to reach the ends of the earth and minister spiritual healing to the multitudes—all to the glory of God.

Focusing on the Facts

1. What do Acts 2:41, 4:4, and 6:7 teach about the early church (see p. 8)?
2. Everything we learn should make us more effective in winning others to Christ because _____ is our _____ (see p. 9).
3. The early church was nurtured in what (see p. 9)?
4. What does Acts 4:32-37 stress? Explain (see p. 10).
5. Why did God discipline Ananias and Sapphira before the whole church (Acts 5:1-11; see p. 10)?
6. To whom has God primarily committed discipline within the church? Explain (see p. 11).
7. Explain the process Jesus gave for dealing with sin in the church (Matt. 18:15-17; see pp. 12-13).
8. Where was Solomon's Porch? Why did it become a gathering place for Christians (see pp. 13-14)?
9. Explain why people who were uncommitted were reluctant to join the church (see p. 14).
10. Why is discipline important in the church (see p. 14)?
11. Explain Jesus' standard for belonging to Him (see pp. 16-17).
12. What was the purpose of the miracles performed by the apostles in Acts? Explain (see pp. 17-18).
13. Are the miracles that occur in Acts 5 supposed to occur today? Explain (see p. 19).

Pondering the Principles

1. In Matthew 18:15-17 the Lord gives us a clear directive for effectively dealing with sin in the lives of others. Unfortunately it is too seldom followed. When a believer knows a brother is in sin, the most common responses are to ignore the problem, to tell one's friends (which is sometimes excused as a prayer request), or to report his sinful actions to the pastor or someone in authority. All those responses are unbiblical. Read Matthew 18:15-17, noting the progression. You may want to memorize verses 15-17, or at least memorize the fact that Matthew 18 contains the biblical process of confronting sin in the church. Ask God to enable you to react biblically the next time you know a brother is in sin. Read Galatians 6:1 to know the proper attitude for carrying out Matthew 18.

2. Although we are responsible to help each other stay pure, Matthew 7:3-5 graphically demonstrates that our first priority is to "cast the beam out of [our] own eye." Before we help others, we should investigate our own condition. Sometimes when we think of personal purity we think of only external behavior. But in 2 Corinthians 7:1 Paul says we should rid ourselves of "all filthiness of the flesh *and spirit*, perfecting holiness in the fear of God" (emphasis added). Are you now guilty of some sin of the flesh or the mind? Have you sinned by what you have said? Stop now and acknowledge your sins to God, asking for His forgiveness and restoration.

2
The Early Church Pattern for Evangelism
—Part 2

Outline

Introduction

Review
I. Purity (vv. 12*b*-14)
II. Power (vv. 12*a*, 15-16)

Lesson
III. Persecution (vv. 17-28)
   A. A Survey of Persecution
      1. Its cause
      2. Its certainty
      3. Its consolation
   B. The Situation in Jerusalem
      1. The leaders' indignation (vv. 17-18)
         a) Its source (v. 17)
         b) Its expression (v. 18)
      2. God's intervention (vv. 19-21*a*)
         a) Illustrated
         b) Explained
            (1) He delivered the disciples (v. 19)
            (2) He directed the disciples (vv. 20-21*a*)
               (*a*) Their mission
               (*b*) Their message
      3. The high priest's investigation (vv. 21*b*-28)
         a) The assembly of the leaders (v. 21*b*)
         b) The absence of the apostles (vv. 22-26)
            (1) Freed from prison (vv. 22-24)
            (2) Found in the Temple (vv. 25-26)

Introduction

Acts 5:12-42 discusses the explosive evangelism of the early church. Although it does not exhaust the subject, it does present five progressive keys to effective evangelism. Evangelism is the responsibility of every Christian. Jesus said His mission was "to seek and to save that which was lost" (Luke 19:10). He commissioned His followers to go "into all the world, and preach the gospel to every creature" (Mark 16:15). Just before His ascension He said to His followers, "Ye shall be witnesses unto me both in Jerusalem, and in all Judaea, and in Samaria, and unto the uttermost part of the earth" (Acts 1:8). Believers are called to reach the world with the truth of Jesus Christ. Most Christians understand that calling and genuinely desire to win people to Christ. However, the outworking of that desire varies greatly. Some believers witness to their friends and loved ones. Others are willing only to pray. Still others merely hope it happens. Regardless of its intensity, I believe every Christian has such a desire.

Review

Acts 5 unveils five keys to effective evangelism.

I. PURITY (vv. 12*b*-14; pp. 10-17)

"They were all with one accord in Solomon's porch. And of the rest dared no man join himself to them; but the people magnified them. And believers were the more added to the Lord, multitudes both of men and women."

In the beginning of chapter 5 Ananias and Sapphira pollute the fellowship by lying to the Holy Spirit (5:1-2). But God purified the church by intervening supernaturally and taking their lives (vv. 3-10). Because that sin had been rooted out, the church was in "one accord" (v. 12). Purity is where evangelism begins. The church that deals with sin is an effective church. Verse 13 says, "Of the rest dared no man join himself to them." That's how the church continued to stay pure. People were aware that the church confronted sin, so they knew not to join if they weren't willing to deal with their sins. Genuine believers were added to the church, attracted by its purity.

II. POWER (vv. 12*a*, 15-16; pp. 17-19)

"By the hands of the apostles were many signs and wonders wrought among the people . . . insomuch that they brought forth the sick into the streets, and laid them on beds and couches, that at the least the shadow of Peter passing by might overshadow some of them. There came also a multitude out of the cities round about unto Jerusalem, bringing sick folks, and them who were vexed with unclean spirits; and they were healed every one."

A pure church has God's power, so its evangelism is effective. God gave the church in Jerusalem the power to work miracles to confirm their preaching. The people of Jerusalem were so convinced those believers had God's power that they put their sick on couches in the streets, hoping that Peter might pass and his shadow heal their diseases. Soon word spread, and people came from all the cities around Jerusalem to be healed—and they all were! The church's power drew people to it; the church's purity allowed them to have that power.

III. PERSECUTION (vv. 17-28)

A. A Survey of Persecution

1. Its cause

Isaiah 14 tells us that Lucifer, an angel, wanted to be like God (vv. 12-14). According to Revelation 12 he led one-third of the angels in a rebellion against God (v. 4). He remains God's antagonist. He is called, among other things, *Satan, the devil,* and *the adversary.* He and his demons, the angels who rebelled with him, were cast out of heaven (vv. 8-9). After his fall Satan came to earth and tempted Eve (Gen. 3:1-5). She and Adam fell (v. 6), and all mankind fell with them (Rom. 5:12). At the present time Satan controls this world. The Bible calls him "the prince [lit., "ruler"] of this world" (John 12:31) and "the prince of the power of the air" (Eph. 2:2). God has temporarily allowed Satan that authority. To some degree every unbeliever is part of Satan's system, which in our society consists primarily of materialism, humanism, and sex. A system run by Satan would naturally be an enemy of God's truth. Satan, his demons, and evil people continually wage war against God, His angels, and His people. Satan's objective is to salvage his authority and continue his rebellion. He was defeated in heaven, but now the earth is his domain. He wants to keep as many people as possible in his system and on his side. When a pure, powerful church wins people to Christ, snatching them out of Satan's control, he becomes irritated and begins persecuting it.

2. Its certainty

Fortunately, whatever Satan tries to do, God uses for His own glory. That's important to know because persecution is inevitable. Second Timothy 3:12 says, "*All* that will live godly in Christ Jesus shall suffer persecution" (emphasis added). If you live a pure, godly life, you will run against the evil world system. Persecution of some form will result. You may be avoided or undermined;

you may face open hostility or violence. Your integrity may be questioned. Or persecution may take the form of subtle insults. A "friend" may suggest that you not talk so much about your faith, commenting that you wouldn't want to be thought of as a religious freak or an obnoxious person. It is true that a Christian should never irritate intentionally or needlessly. But a godly life will always irritate the world, because unholy people don't like holy company. If you're not suffering persecution, you're not living godly. When a pure, powerful church moves out among the world there will be a reaction, because Satan always reacts to purity.

Peter knew about persecution. From the book of Acts we see that he faced it constantly. In 1 Peter 2:20 he says, "If, when ye do well and suffer for it, ye take it patiently, this is acceptable with God." First Peter 3:17 says, "It is better, if the will of God be so, that ye suffer for well-doing than for evil-doing." First Peter 4:14 says, "If ye be reproached for the name of Christ, happy are ye; for the Spirit of glory and of God resteth upon you." In 4:19 he says, "Let them that suffer according to the will of God commit the keeping of their souls to him in well-doing, as unto a faithful Creator." Three times Peter said it is God's will for believers to suffer. Scripture clearly teaches what is God's will for our lives. He wants us to be saved (1 Tim. 2:4), Spirit-filled (Eph. 5:18), sanctified (1 Thess. 4:3), and suffering (1 Peter 4:19). However, our suffering shouldn't be self-inflicted. God doesn't want us to flagellate ourselves. The suffering Peter described is not like that of a man in the Philippines known for crucifying himself every year in an attempt to please God. It is persecution for righteousness' sake, brought on by an evil world offended by true righteousness.

3. Its consolation

One of the Beatitudes is, "Blessed [happy] are they who are persecuted for righteousness' sake; for theirs is the kingdom of heaven. [Happy] are ye, when men shall revile you, and persecute you, and shall say all manner of evil against you falsely, for my sake. Rejoice, and be exceedingly glad; for great is your reward in heaven"

(Matt. 5:10-12). In Romans 8:17 Paul says, "We suffer with him, that we may be also glorified with him." Christians who confront the world with holy, powerful lives, experiencing persecution as a result, will be greatly rewarded in heaven. Scars are the price every godly believer pays for loyalty to Jesus Christ. Second Timothy 3:13 adds that "evil men and seducers shall become worse and worse." Persecution will become more frequent as men become more antagonistic to the gospel.

B. The Situation in Jerusalem

Because so many people were getting saved and being healed (Acts 5:14-16), the believers undoubtedly knew that a second wave of persecution was fast approaching. They probably got excited, remembering the first wave of persecution, which brought about answered prayer, the salvation of many, unification of the church, and, therefore, glory to God (4:23-37).

1. The leaders' indignation (vv. 17-18)

   a) Its source (v. 17)

   "The high priest rose up, and all they that were with him (which is the sect of the Sadducees), and were filled with indignation."

   When the religious leaders of Israel witnessed the miracles and preaching of the Jerusalem church, they got angry. The Greek word translated "indignation" (zalou) speaks of jealousy. They were angry because they were jealous—a typical response for a religious organization that is at odds with God concerning the success of another.

The Sadducees: A Roman Puppet

The Sadducees were a small religious party of wealthy, influential Israelites. The designation "Sadducees" distinguished them from the Pharisees. Whereas the Pharisees were the legalistic conservatives of the New Testament era, the Sadducees were the theologi-

The religious leaders believed they had destroyed Christ's following when they executed Him, but they had only made it grow more quickly. Now thousands of people were claiming to be His followers, and undeniable miracles were occurring throughout the city of Jerusalem. The religious leaders were understandably shaken. Since the Jewish people hated Roman domination and therefore looked for opportunities to incite unrest, the situation in Palestine was volatile. The Sadducees knew that an insurrection would threaten their political clout. Earlier they had warned the disciples against speaking out or teaching in the name of Jesus (4:18). But Peter and John had refused to obey them, saying, "Whether it is right in the sight of God to hearken unto you more than unto God, judge ye" (v. 19). The religious leaders were filled with jealous rage.

b) Its expression (v. 18)

They "laid their hands on the apostles, and put them in the common prison."

Israel's leaders seized them and threw them in jail. How foolish to think that bars could restrict the power of God! They put them in a public ward where all prisoners were confined.

2. God's intervention (vv. 19-21*a*)

a) Illustrated

In Acts 16:12 Paul and Silas arrive in Philippi and begin a fruitful ministry. A certain girl, who was possessed by a demon, was making her masters wealthy by serving as a medium (v. 16). After she had followed Paul for many days, he said to the demon that possessed her, "I command thee, in the name of Jesus Christ, to come out of her" (v. 18). When the demon left her, her powers did also. The girl's masters were enraged that Paul had destroyed their lucrative business. They arrested Paul and Silas and accused them of unlawful teaching (vv. 19-22).

Continuing the narrative, Luke says that when the magistrates "had laid many stripes upon them, they cast them into prison, charging the jailer to keep them safely; who, having received such a charge, thrust them into the inner prison, and made their feet fast in the stocks. And at midnight Paul and Silas prayed, and sang praises unto God; and the prisoners heard them. And suddenly there was a great earthquake, so that the foundations of the prison were shaken; and immediately all the doors were opened, and every one's bands were loosed. And the keeper of the prison, awaking out of his sleep and seeing the prison doors open, drew out his sword and would have killed himself, supposing that the prisoners had been fled. But Paul cried with a loud voice, saying, Do thyself no harm; for we are all here. Then he called for a light, and sprang in, and came trembling, and fell down before Paul and Silas, and brought them out, and said, Sirs, what must I do to be saved?" (vv. 23-30).

The men who imprisoned them believed they had stopped their ministry. Instead, the jailer and his entire family was saved. God always overrules Satan's attempts to thwart His work and uses what Satan meant for evil to accomplish His purposes (cf. Gen. 50:20).

b) Explained

(1) He delivered the disciples (v. 19)

"But an angel of the Lord by night opened the prison doors, and brought them forth."

God sent an angel to free the disciples. It is significant that God didn't use an earthquake, as He did in Acts 16, but an angel instead. Two theological teachings distinguished the Sadducees: they didn't believe in a resurrection—the very thing the disciples were preaching throughout Jerusalem—and they denied the existence of angels (Acts 23:8). God used a being they denied so that the disciples could preach a doctrine they rejected!

(2) He directed the disciples (vv. 20-21*a*)

The angel said, "Go, stand and speak in the temple to the people all the words of this life. And when they heard that, they entered into the temple early in the morning, and taught."

(*a*) Their mission

To the human mind the angel's command does not appear to be the intelligent choice. But God never says we have to understand what He commands—we are simply to obey. Perhaps if we were in that situation we would have preferred to leave Jerusalem for a few weeks until the tension died down. But God said, "Go, stand, and speak." He wants His people to have the courage to tell the truth. The Sadducees kept trying to extinguish the disciples' influence, but doing so was futile. Satan's attempt to extinguish God's work added fuel to the fire.

(*b*) Their message

The phrase "all the words of this life" refers to the gospel. Paul told the Philippians to present "the word of life" (2:16). Jesus entered this world to give life to the spiritually dead. To be spiritually dead is to be unable to sense God, to be unaware of His presence. Regardless of the stimulus, people can't respond to God because they are dead. They grope to find reality when what they really need is life. And Jesus Christ is the only one who can give life. He said, "I am the way, the truth, and the life" (John 14:6). In his first

31

epistle John says, "He that hath the Son hath life" (5:12). When a person is saved, he begins to sense God, to be alive to His world, and becomes a part of what He is and what He's doing. That is life. And Christianity is not just a part of life; it is life. Sometimes people say that Christ is at the center of their lives. I know what they are trying to say, but there's a better way to say it. Christ shouldn't be in the middle of everything; everything should be in Him. He is our life.

The apostles' message was how to have life, and the key to life is the resurrection. Jesus said, "I am the resurrection and the life" (John 11:25). In John 14:19 He tells His disciples, "Because I live, ye shall live also."

The disciples obeyed the angel's command and went into the Temple the next morning and taught.

3. The high priest's investigation (vv. 21b-28)

a) The assembly of the leaders (v. 21b)

"The high priest came, and they that were with him, and called the council together, and all the senate of the children of Israel, and sent to the prison to have them brought."

You can almost picture the austerity of the occasion. Israel's leaders have gathered to deal with these religious upstarts. The "council" refers to the Sanhedrin, the ruling elders of Israel. The "senate" (Gk., *gerousia*) probably refers to the wise, older men who previously had held positions of leadership. It may have consisted primarily of Pharisees, who had previously been in power. The expert advisers of Israel had met to judge those early Christians. They sent to the prison to have the disciples brought before them.

b) The absence of the apostles (vv. 22-26)

32

(1) Freed from prison (vv. 22-24)

"But when the officers came, and found them not in the prison, they returned, and told, saying, The prison truly found we shut with all safety, and the keepers standing outside before the doors; but when we had opened, we found no man within. Now when the high priest and the captain of the temple and the chief priests heard these things, they were perplexed · concerning them, how this would grow."

Witnessing another miracle didn't make the leaders any more ready to believe. Rather it hardened them in their state of unbelief. They were so indifferent that rather than believe the miracle, they dismissed it from their minds, as they had the hundreds of other miracles occurring throughout the city. Verse 24 says that when they heard the apostles were not in the prison, "they were perplexed." The Greek word translated "perplexed" (*diaporeō*) implies that they were at their wits' end. Consider how the religious leaders saw the events of the previous weeks: Israelites who called themselves Christians were disregarding their authority, preaching what they believed to be heresy. Every effort they made to stop the growth of Christianity failed. Indeed, more people were believing every day. They learned that their last attempt—imprisoning the troublemakers —failed. The apostles had disappeared from a locked and guarded cell. It's no surprise that these leaders were on the edge of panic. They turned their energies toward recapturing the prisoners.

(2) Found in the Temple (vv. 25-26)

"Then came one and told them, saying, Behold, the men whom ye put in prison are standing in the temple, and teaching the people. Then went the captain with the officers, and brought them without violence; for they feared the people, lest they should have been stoned."

They found the disciples in the Temple teaching the people. Rather than hiding in the hills, they were doing what they had been told not to do—and people were listening and believing in Christ. Verse 26 says the captain and his officers "brought them without violence." Apparently cooler heads prevailed among the soldiers for the moment, but violence was in them. They restrained it because "they feared the people, lest they should have been stoned" (v. 26). The disciples were content to go with them because they knew that regardless of where they were taken or what happened, God was in charge.

How to React to Persecution from Government

In Acts 5:26 the disciples respond commendably to persecution—with nonresistance. Later in the book of Acts, Paul is on trial before Festus, the Roman governor (chap. 25). The Jews had accused him of "many and grievous complaints . . . which they could not prove" (v. 7). In verse 11 Paul says, "If I . . . am a wrongdoer, and have committed anything worthy of death, I do not refuse to die" (NASB*). If obeying the Lord meant disobeying the government, Paul would do so, willingly accepting the consequences—even if it meant death! That's the right response to persecution. Christians are to obey the government, unless it contradicts a command of God. Then we must obey the Lord and accept the penalty for that decision, even if it be death. Paul was bold in the face of death because he knew that "to live is Christ, and to die is gain" (Phil. 1:21). Death is only a promotion. He continues in verses 23-24, "I am in a strait between two, having a desire to depart and to be with Christ, which is far better. Nevertheless, to abide in the flesh is more needful for you." Christian service gives meaning to our lives on earth.

Because of his appeal to Caesar (Acts 25:11), Paul was sent to Rome. During the journey, there was a shipwreck, but in answer to Paul's prayer no one drowned, giving him the opportunity to declare God's power (27:21-44). Eventually he arrived in Rome (28:15-16), where "he expounded and testified the kingdom of God, persuading [the Jewish leaders] concerning Jesus, both out of the law of Moses, and out of the prophets, from morning till eve-

*New American Standard Bible.

ning" (v. 23). Verses 30-31 say, "Paul dwelt two whole years in his own hired house [a prisoner under house arrest] . . . preaching the kingdom of God, and teaching those things which concern the Lord Jesus Christ." The fruit of his ministry is evident in the letter he wrote from Rome to the Philippians. He said, "All the saints greet you, chiefly they that are of Caesar's household" (4:22). People were constantly being saved because Paul graciously accepted the consequences of choosing to obey the Lord. He displayed the right attitude when facing persecution. That's why when the end was near he was able to say, "I am now ready to be offered" (2 Tim. 4:6).

c) The accusations against the disciples (vv. 27-28)

(1) That they disobeyed the rulers (vv. 27-28*a*)

"When they had brought them, they set them before the council; and the high priest asked them, saying, Did not we strictly command you that ye should not teach in this name?"

That's the first accusation. And it was true. But the disciples had already told them that they would disobey that command. After the religious leaders commanded them not "to speak at all nor teach in the name of Jesus," Peter said, "Whether it is right in the sight of God to hearken unto you more than unto God, judge ye. For we cannot but speak the things which we have seen and heard" (4:18-20).

(2) That they were incriminating the authorities (v. 28*c*)

You "intend to bring this man's blood upon us."

The high priest's second charge was that the disciples had accused Israel of Christ's death, which was an accurate charge. Peter made that indictment repeatedly. In Acts 2:23 he says, "Ye [men of Israel] have taken, and by wicked hands have crucified and slain [Jesus]." In Acts 2:36 he says, "Let all the house of Israel know assuredly, that

35

God hath made that same Jesus, whom ye have crucified, both Lord and Christ." In Acts 3:15 Peter accuses the Israelites of killing the Prince of life. In Acts 4:10 he says, "Be it known unto you all [the Sanhedrin], and to all the people of Israel, that by the name of Jesus Christ of Nazareth, whom ye crucified . . . ." The apostles pronounced them guilty of shedding Christ's blood. Perhaps the Israelites forgot what they had shouted a few weeks before (Matt. 27:25). They were so intent on crucifying Christ that when Pilate refused to take responsibility for His death, the people said, "His blood be on us, and on our children." Peter wasn't accusing them of something they didn't request.

(3) That they were spreading the gospel (v. 28b)

"Behold, ye have filled Jerusalem with your doctrine."

They had accomplished their mission—saturating Jerusalem with the gospel. What a commendation from the Jewish leaders! Notice that the leaders didn't ask about the disciples' miraculous escape. They didn't want to hear about it. Perhaps they were too confused to hear about another miracle.

IV. PERSISTENCE (vv. 29-32)

A. In Obeying God (v. 29)

"Then Peter and the other apostles answered, and said, We ought to obey God rather than men."

The apostles never quit. Even though the high priest had just fired stinging accusations at them, they refused to apologize for the truth. They were tenacious. By saying "we ought to obey God rather than men" Peter was implying that the leaders were opposing God! That is boldness.

B. In Confronting Sin (v. 30)

"The God of our fathers raised up Jesus, whom ye slew and hanged on a tree."

A few moments before, the high priest rebuked Peter and the other disciples for saying Israel's leadership was guilty of Christ's death. Too often after one little skirmish we, as Christ's soldiers, ask for an honorable discharge. But Peter was persistent in his evangelism. He pressed on the sensitive spot, telling the Sanhedrin that they crucified their Messiah. The Greek word translated "slew" (*diacheirizō*) is used only one other time in the New Testament. It means "to murder with one's own hands." Instead of recanting, Peter became more aggressive. He could have said that they crucified Christ, but instead he used the phrase "hanged on a tree." The Old Testament declared that anyone hanged on a tree was cursed (Deut. 21:22-23). Peter was pointing out that the leaders of Israel chose the most shameful, despicable death a man could die for the Son of God—the Messiah of Israel.

C. In Exalting Christ (v. 31)

"Him hath God exalted with his right hand to be a Prince and a Savior, to give repentance to Israel, and forgiveness of sins."

"Right hand" speaks of power. By His power God snatched Christ out of the grave and exalted Him, making Him a prince and a savior. Israel's leaders believed He was insignificant. But God lifted Him up and made Him better than a prince. The Greek word translated "prince" (*archēgos*) speaks of a king or pioneer. Christ offered repentance and forgiveness. Those are inseparable terms, because there's no forgiveness apart from repentance. Often people talk about salvation but leave out repentance. No one is ever saved until he turns from his sin. That doesn't mean he becomes sinless; it means he is sorry for his sin and willing to change. When someone comes to God with a repentant heart, God forgives him.

D. In Upholding Divine Revelation (v. 32)

"We are his witnesses of these things; and so is also the Holy Spirit, whom God hath given to them that obey him."

1. Summarized

The apostles gave witness to what they personally saw and knew, but they also were relating what the Spirit of God was saying through them. In John 14:26 Jesus says to His disciples, "The Comforter, who is the Holy Spirit, whom the Father will send in my name, he shall teach you all things, and bring all things to your remembrance, whatever I have said unto you." He also said, "When they deliver you up, be not anxious how or what ye shall speak; for it shall be given you in that same hour what ye shall speak" (Matt. 10:19). The apostles weren't sharing their own opinions but what the Holy Spirit was telling them. As long as they yielded to the Spirit, they were victorious.

Conclusion

The early church was powerful because it ministered in the energy of the Holy Spirit. Ephesians 6:10 says, "Be strong in the Lord, and in the power of his might." To reach this world for Jesus Christ we must depend on the Spirit of God so that His power flows through us. We can do that only if we're pure.

Focusing on the Facts

1. What was Jesus' mission (Luke 19:10)? Why are believers here (see p. 24)?
2. Why were only genuine believers added to the Jerusalem church (see p. 25)?
3. Who is Lucifer? Why was he cast out of heaven (see p. 26)?
4. Who presently controls the earth and its system? Support your answer with Scripture (see p. 26).
5. What does the evil world system primarily consist of in our society (see p. 26)?

6. What does 2 Timothy 3:12 teach about persecutio (see pp. 26-27)?
7. Explain the consolation of persecution (see pp. 27-.).
8. Why were Israel's leaders angry at the disciples (see p. 28)?
9. Who were the Sadducees (see pp. 28-29)?
10. Why is it significant that God used an angel to free the disciples (see pp. 30-31)?
11. Explain the meaning of the phrase "the words of this life" (see p. 31).
12. Explain what the Bible means when it refers to people as spiritually dead (see p. 31).
13. How should a Christian react to persecution (see pp. 34-35)?
14. What accusations did the high priest make against the disciples (Acts 5:27-28; see pp. 35-36)?
15. Why did Peter say Jesus was "hanged on a tree" (Acts 5:30; see p. 37)?
16. Who did the apostles say empowered their witness (Acts 5:32; see p. 38)?

Pondering the Principles

1. Second Timothy 3:12 tells us that godly living always causes persecution. Perhaps you are suffering persecution now from a coworker, family member, or friend. First consider whether you are being persecuted because of your righteousness or for some less noble reason (cf. 1 Peter 2:19-20; 4:14-16). Have you been proud and condescending toward that unbeliever? Have you been harsh and uncaring? Have you done something to him that he sees as dishonest? If that individual or group is persecuting you for something other than righteousness, immediately seek them out and ask their forgiveness, and if necessary make restitution. Seek to build a bridge of friendship to that person or group. If you discover instead that godliness is the sole reason you are being persecuted, read the book of 1 Peter, giving careful attention to how he says you should respond.

2. The early church was persistent in its evangelism. The believers didn't allow setbacks to extinguish their fervor. After the religious leaders had persecuted the apostles, Peter again told them the gospel of Christ (Acts 5:30-32). Have you given up on someone you want to be saved? Did you allow many months of seemingly unanswered prayer to discourage you? Did that per-

son's negative response cause you not to talk about Christ with him anymore? Ask God to rekindle your desire to see others saved and to give you persistence not to quit. Make a list of lost friends and loved ones whom you used to pray for and witness to but whom you gave up on. Pray for them to be saved. Write or visit them and renew your efforts to reach them.

3
The Early Church Pattern for Evangelism
—Part 3

Outline

Introduction

Review
I. Purity (vv. 12b-14)
II. Power (vv. 12a, 15-16)
III. Persecution (vv. 17-28)
IV. Persistence (vv. 29-32)

A. In Obeying God (v. 29)
B. In Confronting Sin (v. 30)
C. In Exalting Christ (v. 31)
D. In Upholding Divine Revelation (v. 32)
    1. Summarized

Lesson
    2. Specified
        a) As witnesses of Christ (v. 32a)
        b) As messengers of the Holy Spirit (v. 32b)
V. Productivity (vv. 33-42)
    A. The Conviction of the Holy Spirit (v. 33a)
        1. Illustrated
        2. Illuminated
            a) The characteristics of conviction
            b) The goals of conviction
                (1) To convict us of sin
                (2) To convict us of righteousness
                (3) To convict us of judgment

41

Introduction

Everyone has influence: either for good or bad, for life or death. Webster defines influence as "power exerted over the minds or behavior of others." No one exists in isolation. Because we all affect those around us, we need to evaluate our influence.

The influence of the infant church was astonishing. Acts 2:41 says, "They that gladly received his word were baptized; and the same day there were added unto them about three thousand souls." Verse 43 says that "fear came upon every soul." Verse 47 says the church was "having favor with all the people." Acts 3:10 says that after the people saw the lame man healed, "they were filled with wonder and amazement." Verse 11 adds, "As the lame man who was healed held Peter and John, all the people ran together unto them in the porch that is called Solomon's, greatly wondering." Acts 4:4 says, "Many of them who heard the word believed." Acts 4:31-32 says, "When they had prayed, the place was shaken where they were assembled together; and they were all filled with the Holy Spirit, and they spoke the word of God with boldness. And the multitude of those that believed were of one heart and of one soul." Verse 11 of chapter 5 says that after the deaths of Ananias and Sapphira, "Great fear came upon all the church, and upon as many as heard these things." Verses 13-14 note that "of the rest dared no man join himself to them; but the people magnified them. And believers were the more added to the Lord, multitudes both of men and women."

The early church affected its world. Too much of our Christianity stays inside the walls of a building, and there's no influence. But the early church had influence. Their enemies described them as those who had "turned the world upside down" (Acts 17:6). As Christians we all want to have influence—to impact the world for Christ. Acts 5 assists us toward that goal by demonstrating five progressive keys to effective evangelism.

Review

I. PURITY (vv. 12b-14; see pp. 10-17)

II. POWER (vv. 12a, 15-16; see pp. 17-19)

III. PERSECUTION (vv. 17-28; see pp. 26-36)

IV. PERSISTENCE (vv. 29-32)

Proverbs 28:1 says, "The righteous are bold as a lion." Lions have no natural enemies; no animal attacks them, so they are bold. They are called the king of beasts, because no animal can conquer them. Proverbs 28:1 says believers have the same boldness.

A. In Obeying God (v. 29; see p. 36)

B. In Confronting Sin (v. 30; see pp. 36-37)

C. In Exalting Christ (v. 31; see p. 37)

D. In Upholding Divine Revelation (v. 32)

1. Summarized (see pp. 37-38)

Lesson

2. Specified

a) As witnesses of Christ (v. 32a)

"We are his witnesses of these things."

A witness declares what he has experienced. In Acts 1:8 the disciples receive their commission from the Lord: "Ye shall receive power after the Holy Spirit is come upon you; and ye shall be witnesses unto me." They heartily accepted that commission. In Acts 2:32 Peter says, "This Jesus hath God raised up, whereof we all are witnesses." In 10:39 Peter tells Cornelius and those gathered with him, "We are witnesses of all things which [Jesus] did" (cf. 13:31). In verse 41 he describes himself and the other disciples as "witnesses chosen before by God." The apostles knew their task and were obedient to it. Resistance didn't deter them. They used it as an opportunity for more witnessing.

Their clear, precise witness reinforced Israel's guilt. Second Corinthians 13:1 says, "In the mouth of two or three witnesses shall every word be established." Under Old Testament law Israel had to hear the truth from only two or three witnesses. They were responsible to act on that testimony. The Israelites had heard the gospel of Christ from thousands of witnesses. Thus, they were responsible. Addressing the Jewish community, the writer of Hebrews says, "How shall we escape, if we neglect so great salvation, which at the first began to be spoken by the Lord, and was confirmed unto us by them that heard him" (2:3). The Jewish people had heard the truth about Christ from a multitude of witnesses, and it had been confirmed by signs and gifts of the Holy Spirit. Rejecting such overwhelming evidence invited God's judgment. Because the witness is clear, precise, and factual, people are held responsible.

b) As messengers of the Holy Spirit (v. 32*b*)

"So is also the Holy Spirit, whom God hath given to them that obey him."

The disciples were not only witnesses but also messengers, speaking what the Spirit wanted to disclose. When Peter was "filled with the Holy Spirit," he preached (Acts 4:8). Acts 4:31 says, "They were all filled with the Holy Spirit, and they spoke the word of God with boldness." The Spirit of God gave the apostles the words to say. You may think, *If the Holy Spirit gave me the words to say, I could witness too.* You have to read and learn them, but you do have the words of the Holy Spirit—the Bible. Paul told Timothy, "Be diligent to present yourself approved to God as a workman who does not need to be ashamed, handling accurately the word of truth" (2 Tim. 2:15, NASB).

V. PRODUCTIVITY (vv. 33-42)

A church that is pure, powerful, persecuted, and persistent will produce results.

A. The Conviction of the Holy Spirit (v. 33*a*)

"When they heard that, they were cut to the heart."

1. Illustrated

The persistence of the apostles was driving the Jewish leaders into a frenzy. They could not shut them up. The Sanhedrin rebuked them and commanded them to stop preaching. But the disciples refused to obey, vowing to continue being witnesses because God told them to do so. In fact, they kept preaching the very message that cut the religious leaders to the quick—that Israel crucified her own Messiah. The Greek word translated "cut to the heart" (*diapriō*) refers to sawing something in half or being violently agitated. They were gripped both by panic and by the terrible conviction of crucifying their own Messiah. The Word of God always convicts people.

Hebrews 4:12 says, "The word of God is living, and powerful, and sharper than any two-edged sword, piercing even to the dividing asunder of soul and spirit, and of the joints and marrow, and is a discerner of the thoughts and intents of the heart." It's a sword that rips people open with conviction.

The persistent preaching of those early Christians brought about such conviction. They were indicted for the heresy of preaching the resurrection. After their release they continued preaching it, defying the Sadducees' doctrine. They were jailed for preaching, but when an angel released them, they went back to the Temple and preached, defying the Sadducees' authority. They were indicted for accusing the leaders of executing the Messiah, but they reiterated that accusation before the Sanhedrin, defying the Sadducees' spirituality. They were winning converts all over Jerusalem, defying the Sadducees' domination. These religious upstarts had defied the ruling religious party in every possible way. Israel's leaders were violently agitated.

2. Illuminated

   a) The characteristics of conviction

   The English word *conviction* speaks of proving someone guilty. The Greek word translated "to convict" (*elegchō*) occurs seventeen times in the New Testament. It refers to a mental process whereby a person reaches conclusions or views different from those he once held. Ultimately that change in thinking affects how he lives. It is essential to understand that true conviction works in the mind, not the emotions. Much of what we refer to as convicting preaching is purely emotional with little genuine, biblical conviction. Biblical conviction is not spiritual depression or merely feeling sorry that you sinned. True conviction is an awareness that before God you are judicially guilty. Peter's sermons weren't stories designed to manipulate the emotions of the Sanhedrin. His message convicted them of rejecting and executing their Messiah and rebelling against the God of Israel. That's what they needed to know. If conviction is real, it

46

will reach the emotions, but that's not its aim. Preaching must have strong doctrinal content to convict men and women of their sin.

In John 16:7-8 Jesus says, "It is expedient for you that I go away; for if I go not away, the Comforter will not come unto you; but if I depart, I will send him unto you. And when he is come, he will reprove [Gk., *elegchō*] the world." Conviction is the work of the Holy Spirit. He uses the facts of God's Word to produce a change in a man's mind. That change of mind penetrates the emotions and eventually results in a changed life.

b) The goals of conviction

The Holy Spirit convicts people of three things: sin, righteousness, and judgment (John 16:8).

(1) To convict us of sin

In John 16:9 Jesus says the Holy Spirit will convict the world "of sin, because they believe not on me." That verse doesn't say the Spirit will convict the world of its *sins*. You can't convince a man of the seriousness of his sin by talking about his lying, cheating, or adultery. The Holy Spirit convicts a man of the sin of not believing in Jesus Christ. Man needs to be confronted with the fact that having rejected Jesus Christ, he is a rebel and has no reason to expect anything from God but punishment. That's why Peter told the Israelites that although they killed Christ, God raised Him. He was showing that they were in opposition to God. Even though they claimed to be the people of God, they weren't even near Him, because they had not acknowledged Jesus as Messiah. True conviction makes a man conscious of the damning sin of rejecting Christ.

(2) To convict us of righteousness

In verse 10 Jesus says the Spirit also will convict "of righteousness, because I go to my Father, and ye see me no more." Only righteous people are allowed to enter the presence of the Father. However, the world has a totally confused sense of righteousness. For example, the Israelites killed Jesus in the name of righteousness although He was the only truly righteous one. They judged Him to be an unrighteous criminal, worthy of death. But God exalted Him, thereby declaring Christ's righteousness to the world, regardless of their verdict. Man needs to be convinced that Jesus is righteous, the proof of which is His resurrection and ascension. That's why Jesus said, "I go to my Father, and ye see me no more." The fact that He entered God's presence proves His righteousness.

(3) To convict us of judgment

In verse 11 Jesus says the Spirit will also convict "of judgment, because the prince of this world is judged." Man must understand that if he doesn't come to Christ but lives in constant rebellion against Him, he will be judged. The guarantee that everyone who denies Christ will be judged is the judgment of Satan. Satan can be thought of as a kind of firstfruits of judgment. If someone as powerful as Satan was judged, how can any lesser rebel escape punishment? Satan's judgment came at the cross, even though he was thrown out of heaven long before. If God judged the second most powerful being in the universe, condemning him to dwell forever in the Lake of Fire, no other rebel can elude judgment.

Men need to be convicted of the serious sin of not believing in Christ. They need to realize that they have a reverse system of righteousness and know that judgment is inevitable for anyone who rejects Christ. We see that true conviction is based on theology, which is exactly what you find in Peter's messages.

B. The Varying Reactions of People (vv. 33b-42)

Whenever preaching produces conviction, people react primarily in one of three ways: violent hostility, tolerant indecision, or saving acceptance.

1. Violent hostility (v. 33b)

"[They] took counsel to slay them."

The Sadducees saw only one thing to do: kill the disciples. How could they conclude that in the face of all the evidence? Verse 16 indicates that every sick and demon-possessed person that came into Jerusalem seeking healing was made well. Yet the Sadducees blinded themselves to reality because of their hard-hearted unbelief and decided to kill those who were doing so much good. That's a ridiculous but common reaction. Instead of yielding to truth, they would have compounded their sin by killing those who were sharing the good news of God's forgiveness.

In Acts 9 Paul goes to Damascus to arrest Christians but is saved on the road outside the city. Acts 9:22-23 says he "increased the more in strength, and confounded the Jews who dwelt at Damascus, proving that this is very Christ. And after many days were fulfilled, the Jews took council to kill him." The righteousness of those who know God offends wicked people. In Matthew 10:21-22 Jesus says, "The brother shall deliver up the brother to death, and the father the child; and the children shall rise up against their parents, and cause them to be put to death. And ye shall be hated of all men, for my name's sake, but he that endureth to the end shall be saved."

In Matthew 23:34-38 Christ, speaking to the leaders of Israel, says, "Behold, I send unto you prophets, and wise men, and scribes; and some of them ye shall kill and crucify, and some of them shall ye scourge in your synagogues, and persecute them from city to city, that upon you may come all the righteous blood shed upon the earth, from the blood of righteous Abel unto the blood of Zechariah, son of Barachiah, whom ye slew between the temple and the altar. Verily I say unto you, All these things shall come upon this generation [this was fulfilled in A.D. 70 in the destruction of Jerusalem]. O Jerusalem, Jerusalem, thou that killest the prophets, and stonest them who are sent unto thee, how often would I have gathered thy children together, even as a hen gathereth her chickens under her wings, and ye would not! Behold, your house is left unto you desolate."

The religious leaders tried to kill Jesus throughout His public ministry. John 5:16, 7:32, 8:59, 10:31, and 11:57 underscore their desire to extinguish His ministry at all costs. Finally they nailed Him to a cross. Jesus told His disciples that they could expect the same treatment because they were His representatives (John 15:20-21). Some people are still violently opposed to Christianity, and that's as it should be. What we say and how we live should be so clear that the world has to notice, whether they like it or not. If our gospel message is convicting enough to anger people, it's also convicting enough to point them to salvation.

2. Tolerant indecision (vv. 34-40)

   a) Gamaliel's counsel (vv. 34-39)

      (1) The man (v. 34)

          "Then stood there up one in the council, a Pharisee, named Gamaliel, a teacher of the law, held in reputation among all the people, and commanded to put the apostles forth a little space."

      (a) A member of the Pharisees

          There were Pharisees within the Sanhedrin, the seventy-member council that led Israel, but the Sadducees controlled it. The Sadducees could maintain that control because they were wealthy and had allied themselves with Rome. They had two primary concerns: Greek

50

customs and peaceful relations with the Romans. They were theological liberals, rejecting the concepts of resurrection and angelic beings.

The Pharisees were political traditionalists, purists regarding the law, and nationalistic. They believed so strongly that Israel should exist apart from Rome's authority they were willing to participate in rebellion. They strongly denounced the Sadducees for collaborating with Rome for political and economic advantage. Much like the dichotomy between evangelicals and liberals today, those two groups were poles apart.

The Sadducees were influential with the Sanhedrin and with Rome but exercised little influence on the populace. The Pharisees swayed the people. Josephus, the first-century Jewish historian, said that the Sadducees would often acquiesce to the demands of the Pharisees because of their popularity (*Antiquities* 18.1.4). That's what is happening in Acts 5. The people were open to Christianity because their friends and family members were being healed. The Pharisees knew that if they were to persecute the Christians, they would lose favor with the people, so they were determined not to do that. The Sadducees knew that the people respected the Pharisees, so they frequently capitulated to them, wanting the people's favor. Rabbi Gamaliel, knowing all this, stood to speak. Since he was a Pharisee, he had the people on his side, so the Sadducees had to listen. He didn't want the Christians to die. His reason was probably political even though it is heavily disguised in theological garb.

(*b*) A teacher of the law

Verse 34 says he was "a teacher of the law." The Talmud, the rabbinical writings of Ju-

daism, calls him "Rabban Gamaliel the Elder." *Rabban* was reserved for the most emi-
nent teachers of Israel (cf. John 20:16). Tradition
states that he was the grandson of Hillel, one
of Israel's greatest teachers. Speaking of his
death in A.D. 52 the Talmud says, "When Rabban Gamaliel the Elder died, regard for the
Torah [the study of the Law] ceased, and purity and piety died" (end of *Sotah*). The apostle Paul once studied under Gamaliel (Acts
22:3). He was one of the greatest teachers of
Judaism who ever lived. Because of Gamaliel's personal reputation and his being a
Pharisee, his views would be heard.

(2) The message (vv. 35-39)

(*a*) His exhortation (v. 35)

"[He] said unto them, Ye men of Israel, take
heed to yourselves what ye intend to do as
touching these men."

Gamaliel advised his colleagues to be cau-
tious. The Pharisees believed strongly that
God Himself would deal with problems and
that He didn't need man's help. That was the
theological supposition behind Gamaliel's advice.

(*b*) His illustrations (vv. 36-37)

"Before these days rose up Theudas, boasting
himself to be somebody, to whom a number
of men, about four hundred, joined themselves; who was slain, and all, as many as
obeyed him, were scattered, and brought to
nothing. After this man rose up Judas of Galilee in the days of the registration, and drew
away many people after him; he also per-
ished, and all, even as many as obeyed him,
were dispersed."

Gamaliel gave his associates two illustrations of how God deals with those who oppose Him. Scholars aren't certain who Theudas was. Josephus mentions a Theudas involved with rebellion, but his was different from what is described here and occurred many years later. Gamaliel's point is that Theudas rose to popularity and faded into obscurity without Israel's leaders doing anything.

After the death of Herod the Great in 4 B.C., thousands of robbers marauded Palestine. Some of those robbers formed groups, crowned their leaders kings, and started various revolutions. Such was the case of Judas of Galilee. He led a rebellion in A.D. 6 during the census and taxation under Quirinius. Judas argued that because God is king, paying taxes to Rome was blaspheming God. The Roman government was intolerant of such rebellion and successfully ended Judas's revolt. Gamaliel says that "all, even as many as obeyed him, were dispersed" (v. 37). That wasn't entirely accurate, however, because Judas's rebellion spawned a group that later became known as the Zealots. The Zealots were an extremely nationalistic group of Israelites whose influence was still felt in Israel during Gamaliel's lifetime. Judas wasn't as ineffective as Gamaliel said. (In fact, Josephus implied that the spirit of rebellion against taxation fostered by Judas is what led to the downfall of Jerusalem in A.D. 70 [*Antiquities* 18.1.1., 6; 20.5.2].)

(c) His point (vv. 38-39)

"Now I say unto you, Refrain from these men, and let them alone; for if this counsel or this work be of men, it will come to nothing; but if it be of God, ye cannot overthrow it, lest perhaps ye be found even to fight against God."

This is the conclusion he's making from those illustrations: whatever succeeds is of God; whatever fails is not—a fallacious principle in a fallen world. God allows evil to exist. Gamaliel's principle will come true only when Christ returns to establish His kingdom on earth, thus reversing the curse.

Gamaliel's principle can't be used to evaluate what's happening now. Many things that God hates are successful. For example, the Sanhedrin was still an active religious force in Israel although it was instrumental in Christ's death. Today there are tremendously successful movements that God has nothing to do with. Gamaliel's idea was to wait and see. He witnessed the healings and miracles. He knew of the resurrection of Jesus Christ and His empty grave. What was he waiting to see? What more did he need to see?

The only way to judge something accurately is by comparing it with Scripture. If Gamaliel were a true teacher of Israel, he should have recommended that the council study the Old Testament text to see if the new teaching was biblical. But he was a pseudo-scholar. Jesus said, "O foolish ones, and slow of heart to believe all that the prophets have spoken!" (Luke 24:25). A master of Scripture would have known that Jesus fulfilled every messianic prophecy. Instead Gamaliel made a weak application of poor theology.

"If it be of God, ye cannot overthrow it" (v. 39) is his only valid conclusion. Many people have tried to overthrow that which is of God but instead have been crushed by it. In Matthew 12:30 Jesus says, "He that is not with me is against me." People fight God. They oppose His gospel, His Word, His providence, and His Spirit's conviction. But no one defeats Him.

Today Is the Day of Salvation

Many people today hide the same way Gamaliel did—waiting to see. They aren't quite ready to follow Jesus Christ. The apostle Paul knew more than his teacher. He said, "Behold, *now* is the accepted time; behold, *now* is the day of salvation" (2 Cor. 6:2, emphasis added). That is Paul's way of saying, "Don't just wait and see." On the night of October 8, 1871, Dwight L. Moody was preaching in Chicago and told his audience to go home and think about what he had said about the claims of Christ. That was the night of the great Chicago fire. Half his congregation died. Moody never again told anyone to wait.

b) The Sanhedrin's consent (v. 40)

> "To him they agreed; and when they had called the apostles, and beaten them, they commanded that they should not speak in the name of Jesus, and let them go."

After listening to Gamaliel, the council agreed with him and decided to follow his advice. But there was so much animosity in their hearts, they beat each of the apostles with thirty-nine stripes (cf. Deut. 25:1-3; 2 Cor. 11:24). The Talmud tells us that the hands of the victim would be tied to a post. His shirt would be removed. The man wielding the whip stood on a stone behind him and was required to swing as hard as he could. He used two wide, thick pieces of leather about four feet long. One-third of the stripes were given on the front of the victim and two-thirds on his back. Each of the apostles was beaten in that fashion (*Makkoth* 22b).

3. Saving acceptance (vv. 41-42)

> "They departed from the presence of the council, rejoicing that they were counted worthy to suffer shame for his name. And daily in the temple, and in every house, they ceased not to teach and preach Jesus Christ."

The disciples rejoiced that they had been considered worthy to suffer for Christ, who had suffered for them.

Like Paul, they bore in their bodies "the marks of the Lord Jesus" (Gal. 6:17)—blows that had been meant for Him. When the world persecutes a believer, they're after Christ, so that believer is filling up in his body "the afflictions of Christ" (Col. 1:24). But the disciples didn't stop preaching Jesus Christ. And the results were amazing. Acts 6:1 says that "in those days . . . the number of the disciples was multiplied."

Conclusion

We tire and quit. We become exhausted merely putting on our armor. As veterans of a few skirmishes, we seek an honorable discharge—but the early church didn't. They kept at their task and turned their world upside down. The principles of effective evangelism are all here in Acts 5: purity, power, persecution, persistence, and productivity.

Focusing on the Facts

1. What did the disciples' clear, factual witness do to Israel? Explain (Acts 5:33; see p. 44).
2. Explain how the Holy Spirit gives us His words today (see p. 45).
3. Define *diapriō*. Why were Israel's leaders in that condition (see p. 45)?
4. What are the characteristics of conviction (see pp. 46-47)?
5. The Holy Spirit convicts people of what? Explain each (John 16:9; see pp. 47-48).
6. True conviction makes a man conscious of the damning sin of _____ _____ (see p. 47).
7. What is the ultimate proof of Christ's righteousness (see p. 48)?
8. What is the guarantee that all who reject Christ will be judged (see p. 48)?
9. Did Christ predict that the disciples would face violent hostility? Support your answer with Scripture (see pp. 49-50).
10. Explain the differences between the Sadducees and the Pharisees (see p. 51).
11. Explain the power struggle between those two parties in Acts 5 (see p. 51).

12. Describe Gamaliel (see p. 52).
13. What theological supposition was behind Gamaliel's advice (see p. 52)?
14. Who were the Zealots? How did they arise (see p. 53)?
15. What principle did Gamaliel draw from his illustrations? Is it valid? Explain (see pp. 53-54).
16. Describe the beating the apostles received (see p. 55).
17. Explain how Galatians 6:17 and Colossians 1:24 apply to suffering Christians (see p. 56).

Pondering the Principles

1. Gamaliel was obviously knowledgeable about Scripture. But when he should have relied on it as the judge of truth, he arrived at his own conclusions, which proved to be fallacious. As a teacher of the law, he should have compared the apostles' teaching to the Old Testament text, and then come to a conclusion. Have you allowed tradition or pet systems of interpreting the Bible to have precedence over clear biblical teaching? Do you automatically assume a teaching is wrong if it is contrary to what you've always been taught? Determine to let the Bible say what it says and not read in your own interpretations. Ask God to teach you the truth of His Word by His Spirit.

2. If Christians are not aware of the different reactions people have to the gospel, they can easily become discouraged about witnessing for Christ. Review the ways the people in Acts 5 responded to the gospel (see pp. 49-56). Think of incidents in which someone responded to your witness in each of those ways. To gain further insight into man's reaction to the gospel, read the parable of the soils in Luke 8:4-15. Notice that in only one case out of four was the response to Christ's ministry saving acceptance. Our responsibility is to sow the seed, not to make it take root (cf. 1 Cor. 3:5-7). When you witness, be mentally prepared to see one of those reactions. Ask God for the courage to witness for Christ regardless of how people respond.

4
Spiritual Organization

Outline

Introduction
A. Maintaining a Balance
B. Assisting the Spirit
C. Establishing the Framework

Lesson
I. The Reasons for Spiritual Organization (vv. 1-2, 4)
   A. Growth of the Church (v. 1a)
     1. Jewish expansion continues
     2. Gentile evangelism begins
   B. Dissension Among the People (v. 1b-c)
     1. Because of Satan's effort
       a) Persecution
       b) Contamination
       c) Dissension
     2. Because of natural divisions (v. 1b)
     3. Because of neglected needs (v. 1c)
   C. The Details of Ministry (v. 2)
   D. The Priorities of the Apostles (v. 4)
     1. Their clarification
     2. Their commitment
       a) Paul's example of commitment
       b) Paul's instructions to Timothy
       c) Paul's discussion about salary
II. The Requirements for Church Leadership (v. 3)
   A. That They Be Men
   B. That They Be Church Members
   C. That They Have a Good Reputation
   D. That They Be Spiritual
   E. That They Be Wise

III. The Roster of Those Selected (v. 5)

IV. The Results of Spiritual Organization (vv. 6-7)

Introduction

Acts 6:1-7 is foundational for understanding proper church organization.

A. Maintaining a Balance

Some people believe that when Christians get organized, they become unchristian. They point out that the New Testament church is an organism: its life is its connection to Christ. But to conclude that the church is an organism and cannot be organized is wrong; to say it is only an organization and shouldn't be a functioning, living entity is wrong. The early church was an organized organism. All organisms that function correctly are organized—they function in an ordered sequence. Even our bodies are organized. Paul commanded the Corinthians to "let all things be done decently and in order" (1 Cor. 14:40).

In Acts 6 we see the early church as an effective organism in need of better organization. They had greatly influenced the Jewish community in Jerusalem, astounding people with miracles and signs. Multitudes had come to Christ. Believers were sharing their possessions with others in a spirit of love. The church was a beautifully functioning organism. But the Holy Spirit knew it needed better organization, so He used a crisis to start that process.

B. Assisting the Spirit

Biblical church organization always assists ministries that the Spirit has already begun. In Scripture the church, like an organism, begins to live, move, and develop ministries. Then the church builds a framework around those ministries so they can function smoothly. The early church's evangelism was mushrooming. But it reached a plateau where it needed better structure to evangelize more effectively. Effective organization accommodates God's Spirit so whatever ministry believers want to pursue can be done smoothly and with the greatest benefit.

C. Establishing the Framework

The Jerusalem church already had the seeds of organization. The early chapters of Acts mention several times the number of believers there were, implying that someone kept records of the membership (cf. 2:41; 4:4). The early church also had certain times and places to meet for public worship, prayer, and study of the Word (cf. 2:46; 3:1). Acts 2:46 says the believers were "breaking bread from house to house." According to Acts 4:32-35, money and goods were collected and distributed to meet everyone's needs. All those activities require organization and someone to administer them. Organizing programs and schemes and then finding people to do them isn't the responsibility of the church leaders. They should keep teaching the Word, and, when people want to start a new ministry, the leaders should give them a framework in which to minister. The organization of the early church was simple: the apostles taught and ruled, and everyone else carried out what they said. As the church grew, an organizational crisis arose. But the early church was willing to organize itself as its life and growth demanded. Giving structure to current ministries and eliminating current problems are the essence of organization.

Lesson

Acts 6:1-7 gives us insight into four important considerations at the first recorded organizational meeting of the church.

I. THE REASONS FOR SPIRITUAL ORGANIZATION (vv. 1-2, 4)

"In those days, when the number of the disciples was multiplied, there arose a murmuring of the Grecians against the Hebrews, because their widows were neglected in the daily ministration. Then the twelve called the multitude of the disciples unto them, and said, It is not fitting that we should leave

the word of God, and serve tables . . . but we will give ourselves continually to prayer, and to the ministry of the word."

A. Growth of the Church (v. 1a)

"In those days, when the number of the disciples was multiplied."

1. Jewish expansion continues

Although we don't know exactly how large the church
had grown, it may well have been between twenty and
thirty thousand. And the church was only a few months
old at this point! They hadn't had time to adjust to their
growth, and they were faced with the logistical impossi-
bility of ministering effectively to all those people. Someone had to insure that the poor received the food they
needed. Someone had to oversee the collection and the
distribution of it to those who were in need. Another
person had to supervise gathering the elements for the
Lord's Table and figuring how many people to prepare
for. Someone else needed to take care of the details of
baptism, such as locating an appropriate place. Someone had to make sure the people knew when and where
the meetings would be held and to ask someone to teach
at each meeting. With all that to oversee, the apostles
were becoming overloaded.

2. Gentile evangelism begins

The apostles had accomplished the first part of the goal
Christ gave them when He said, "Ye shall be witnesses
unto me both in Jerusalem, and in all Judaea, and in Samaria, and unto the uttermost part of the earth" (Acts
1:8). Acts 5:28 indicates their ministry had permeated Jerusalem. Now they were ready to move out to Judea,
Samaria, and the world. Before that began, they needed
a framework on which they could expand. In the next
chapters Luke introduces Paul, whose ministry was primarily to the Gentiles. The church was on the threshold
of taking the gospel to Gentiles. But only a united
church is effective in evangelism. The early church
needed more organization.

B. Dissension Among the People (v. 1*b-c*)

1. Because of Satan's effort

   Whenever someone begins to accomplish something for God, Satan intensifies his attempts to stop it. There are three tactics Satan used against the early church and still uses today.

   a) Persecution

   Whether he uses emotional, mental, or physical persecution, Satan tries to unnerve Christians and to convince them to withdraw from the spiritual battle. Much of the ministry of church leadership is spent encouraging saints to be bold in communicating Christ. Some saints always linger in the shadows. You urge them to become involved in reaching the world. But Satan causes resistance, and they retreat. Because persecution can be so effective, he continues to use it. However, he tried it against the early church, and it didn't work. The church grew faster, and God worked even more miracles, proving that Jesus was Messiah. Every time Satan persecuted the church, God overruled.

   b) Contamination

   Satan's second approach is within the church itself. If he can tempt a believer to sin, he can pollute the Body of Christ. Satan tried that with Ananias and Sapphira. But God purified the church by taking their lives. Their fate motivated other Christians to stay pure and kept those who were insincere from joining. Satan used sin in the Body to restrain the gospel, but God dealt with the sin, and the gospel spread faster.

   c) Dissension

   Satan's third tactic to cripple the church is getting believers to fight each other. When he succeeds, hypocrisy dilutes the church's message, and internal conflict saps its power. Because of petty issues, discontent, gossip, and power struggles among their members, many churches use all their spiritual resources to stop fights rather than to fulfill the commission of the Lord. Dissension makes effective evangelism impossible.

Satan still uses those same tactics. Yet believers continue to fall prey to him. If a football team had only three plays, it wouldn't be too effective, because its opponent would know what play was going to be run and prepare to stop it. The church knows what Satan's going to do but still lets him do it. Too often when Satan tries to make us fearful by persecution, we become afraid and muffle our message. When he attempts to pollute the church by tempting us to sin, we all too easily give in. When he works to create dissensions, we get caught up in petty disputes, arguments, and bickering. Satan's attacks can be discouraging. But they can also be an exciting challenge, because you can win a victory only if you're in a battle. The struggle allows us to see God demonstrate His power. The church should strive to encourage the persecuted, deal with those who pollute the fellowship by their sin, and help the divisive to love.

2. Because of natural divisions (v. 1*b*)

"There arose a murmuring of the Grecians against the Hebrews."

The early church preached the gospel primarily to Israelites. Eventually the apostle Paul would orchestrate the church's first concerted effort to reach Gentiles with the gospel. The church in Jerusalem consisted primarily of two groups of Israelites: native-born Palestinians, whom Luke calls "Hebrews," and Hellenistic Israelites, who had lived in places such as Asia Minor and North Africa. These are the "Grecians." Some Hellenistic families had lived out of Palestine for three or four generations, but many maintained their Jewish heritage. Some even returned to Jerusalem for the Jewish feasts. Many Hellenistic Jews were saved on the Day of Pentecost. The church was composed of native Israelites and Jewish people who were born and raised outside the land. Since the Hebrews spoke Aramaic and the Grecians spoke Greek, they broke into groups where they could communicate, thus creating a natural division. In addition, the native Israelites tended to treat the Hellenistic Jews with a degree of contempt, because they believed they weren't true Hebrews. They believed they were disloyal to the land and were polluted by Greek culture.

3. Because of neglected needs (v. 1c)

"Because their widows were neglected in the daily ministration."

The Grecians believed the church was slighting their widows when it dispensed food and money. Perhaps the native Israelites had a tendency to overlook them because there were fewer of them and the language barrier may have made the Grecian widows keep to themselves. A complaint arose. Caring for widows and the poor has always been a Jewish custom. Commentator William Barclay tells us that in the synagogue there were officials known as receivers of alms. Every Friday morning they went to the marketplace and from house to house to collect an offering. Later that same day the poor and the widows received that offering. Those with temporary shortages received enough to get them through their difficulty. Those who needed regular support received enough for fourteen meals, two meals a day until the following Friday (*The Acts of the Apostles* [Philadelphia: Westminister, 1955], p. 50). It was customary for the Jewish people to care for the poor and the widows in that way.

In 1 Timothy 5:3-16 Paul specifically defines such provision as the church's responsibility. Each church should care for the widows of the congregation who don't have enough to live on. That is our wonderful privilege and responsibility, every bit as binding on churches in the present as it was in the past. However, the Grecian widows weren't receiving what the Lord designed for the church to provide, so murmuring began. Because lingual and cultural barriers already divided the two groups, this issue could have driven a wedge between them and spread a black cloud over the beginning of Christianity.

65

C. The Details of Ministry (v. 2)

"Then the twelve called the multitude of the disciples unto them, and said, It is not fitting that we should leave the word of God, and serve tables."

The apostles didn't deny that the Grecian widows were being neglected. They saw the problem but knew they would have to leave the Word of God if they were to care for the widows themselves. Their calling was to the preaching of the Word, and they didn't want to neglect that. The Greek word translated "tables" (*trapeza*) is used to refer to meals and even the tables that the moneychangers used in Matthew 21:12. It's a broad word, referring to many of the ministries of the early church, such as serving a meal when the believers gathered to eat, doling out money to the needy for necessities, or collecting funds. The disciples found it impossible to accomplish all those details of ministry. Distributing money and food to the needy and handling the business of the church are good and honorable activities. But God called the disciples to the ministry of the Word, and that needed to be their priority.

How Organized Should the Church Be?

The debate about church organization has reached a zenith in our times. At one end of the spectrum there is the church that resembles a well-organized, well-staffed, efficient corporation. On the other end are those who emphasize small, home Bible studies and the life of the Body. Some Christians believe the church should have no formal organization—that it shouldn't own a building or piece of property or have any paid staff responsible for particular duties. I heard one such person say that no organization or system can be of God. However, God is the most organized being in the universe! Every dimension of God's world is organized. To say that an organized church can't be of God misconstrues God's nature, which is the pinnacle of organization. The Old Testament records God's covenant with Israel, which is a system from beginning to end.

On the other hand, some people say the church is only an organization. Therefore it must be run like a business. First they develop a complex organizational structure with boards, committees, and subcommittees. Then they ask the Holy Spirit to bless their efforts and operate within that detailed organizational structure. It is equally foolish to ask the Holy Spirit to work without giving Him a structure in which to operate. Both extremes are wrong.

The work of the ministry had grown to such proportions that the twelve would have had to neglect the Word of God to accomplish it. Someone needed to oversee the work and mobilize the people to carry it out.

A Crisis Among Pastors

The disciples said, "It is not fitting that we should leave the word of God" (v. 2). Unfortunately, many men in the ministry today are busy doing everything but what God said was to be their priority—the ministry of the Word of God. This problem has reached crisis proportions. Pastors, teachers, missionaries, and evangelists are easily distracted from the Word to "serve tables." Congregations languish in spiritual infancy year after year, never having real spiritual food. Often the pastors are wonderful people, but they have been unwittingly pushed into those distractions by a congregation that has unbiblical expectations. The apostles knew why they had been given to the church—to teach the Word of God—and refused to neglect it because other responsibilities demanded their time.

D. The Priorities of the Apostles (v. 4)

"But we will give ourselves continually to prayer, and to the ministry of the word."

1. Their clarification

The disciples determined to focus on praying and preaching. The same Greek word (*diakonia*) is translated "serve" in verse 2 and "ministry" in verse 4. They were saying, "We'll serve the Word; you serve the tables." Ephesians 4:11-12 says that the Lord gave apostles, teaching pastors, and evangelists to the church to perfect the saints so they could do the work of the ministry. Leaders are to bring people to maturity so they can minister. The apostles determined not to let any service take precedence over prayer and the ministry of the Word. That was their priority. One of the church's primary tasks is to teach the Word of God as it should be taught —not presenting platitudes about the Bible or stories about spiritual fruit, but unfolding the text. However, preaching without prayer is shallow and dry. We must pray constantly for those to whom we preach and for ourselves, that God would make us useful vessels.

2. Their commitment

The Bible teaches that the man God calls to shepherd the flock must give himself wholly to prayer and preaching. Living by those priorities requires total commitment. The phrase "give ourselves continually" stresses the disciples' commitment. Ministering like that demands everything you are; it demands that you saturate yourself with the Word of God. The story is told that once after a great Bible teacher had finished teaching, a young man approached him and said, "I'd give the world to teach the Bible like you do." The teacher replied, "That's exactly what it will cost you."

a) Paul's example of commitment

The apostle Paul knew about absolute and incessant commitment to the Word. Acts 20:17-20, speaking of Paul, says, "From Miletus he sent to Ephesus, and called the elders of the church. And when they were come to him, he said unto them, Ye know, from the first day that I came into Asia, after what manner I have been with you at all seasons, serving the Lord with all humility of mind, and with many tears, and trials, which befell me by the lying in wait of the Jews; and how I kept back nothing that was profitable unto you, but have shown you, and have taught you publicly, and from house to house." Acts 28:30-31 indicates that Paul taught the Bible constantly for two years while under house arrest in Rome. Although Paul was immersed in teaching the Word, he had a personable, warm heart that loved people. He had many close personal relationships. Timothy in particular was his special friend. Paul reveals his heart when he speaks to Timothy. In 2 Timothy 4:9 Paul says to him, "Do thy diligence to come shortly unto me." In verse 21 he adds, "Do thy diligence to come before winter." With much pathos he says, "Demas hath forsaken me, having loved this present world" (v. 10). Paul ministered on a personal basis, but his primary commitment to the church was teaching and preaching the Word of God.

The disciples' commitment to the Word is a pattern we must imitate in our ministries today. Such commitment will require diligent study even when we don't feel like it. Paul described his compulsion to preach the Word this way: "Woe is unto me, if I preach not the gospel!" (1 Cor. 9:16). But our flesh knows that such commitment involves pain and self-discipline and rebels against it. Biblical ministry demands total commitment.

b) Paul's instructions to Timothy

Paul told Timothy his ministry was to "command and teach" (1 Tim. 4:11). In verse 13 he says, "Till I come, give attendance to reading, to exhortation, to doctrine." That refers to reading the text, explaining the text, and applying the text—a good definition of expository preaching. In verses 14-16 Paul says, "Neglect not the gift that is in thee . . . . Meditate upon these things; give thyself wholly to them, that thy profiting may appear to all. Take heed unto thyself and unto the doctrine." Timothy was to give special attention to two things: himself and his teaching. He needed to have a pure life, or what he said would have no meaning. That's why Paul said, "Be thou an example of the believers, in word, in conduct, in love, in spirit, in faith, in purity" (v. 12). Paul summarizes the ministerial command in 2 Timothy 4:2, where he says, "Preach the word."

c) Paul's discussion about salary

Ministering the Word requires such total commitment that those who do so shouldn't be encumbered with earning a separate living. First Corinthians 9:14 says, "Even so hath the Lord ordained that they who preach the gospel should live of the gospel." The context pertains to paying the preacher. Notice verse 11: "If we have sown unto you spiritual things, is it a great thing if we shall reap your carnal things?" If someone teaches you God's Word, you should care for his material needs. Galatians 6:6 says, "Let the one who is taught the word share all good things with him who teaches" (NASB). These commands to provide for the needs of those who teach God's Word illustrate how preoccupied the preacher should be with study and preaching. That's why the disciples said, "We will give ourselves continually to prayer and to the ministry of the word" (Acts 6:4).

II. THE REQUIREMENTS FOR CHURCH LEADERSHIP (v. 3)

"Wherefore, brethren, look among you for seven men of honest report, full of the Holy Spirit and wisdom, whom we may appoint over this business."

In addition to being saved, there are five basic requirements for church leaders.

A. That They Be Men

"Men."

The leaders within the church are to be men. That doesn't imply a lack of spiritual equality (cf. Gal. 3:28). God has used women throughout church history. The New Testament mentions Dorcas (Acts 9:36-39), Lydia (Acts 16:14-15), Phoebe (Rom. 16:1-2), Priscilla (Acts 18:2-3, 18, 26; Rom. 16:3; 1 Cor. 16:19), and the daughters of Philip (Acts 21:8-9). God still uses women. Titus 2:4-5 commands women to instruct younger women to "be sober-minded, to love their husbands, to love their children, to be discreet, chaste, keepers at home, good, obedient to their own husbands, that the word of God be not blasphemed." Women have great responsibilities and are in many ways the warmth and depth of the church. But God's basic instruc-

70

tion plan of operation in the church is for the men to be in authority.

B. That They Be Church Members

"Among you."

God expects a church to find its leadership from within its own ranks. Often churches become frustrated looking for leadership in other churches. Some look nationwide for pastors and assistants to fill a need when they could have—and should have—examined their own membership. In every church where the Bible is accurately taught and its authority obeyed, you can count on God to mature the saints and raise them up to serve within that church. As a good general rule, the leadership of a church should come from within itself.

C. That They Have a Good Reputation

"Of honest report."

The church's leaders must have a good reputation. They should be men whose integrity and reputation is blameless, not only among the church but also in the eyes of the unbelieving world (1 Tim. 3:7).

D. That They Be Spiritual

"Full of the Holy Spirit."

They must be spiritual men. Being filled with the Spirit means being controlled by the Spirit. Church leaders should be men whose lives are not their own but are devoted to the will of God.

E. That They Be Wise

"[Full of] wisdom."

Lastly, the officers of the church must be wise.

Were the Men Selected in Acts 6 Deacons?

Although many Christians consider the men in Acts 6 to be the first deacons, there is evidence to the contrary. This chapter is simply recording the beginnings of church leadership. These men were all the organization the church needed at that time. Later Paul divided church leadership into three distinct offices: elders, deacons, and deaconesses (1 Tim. 3). The ministries of Stephen and Philip, two of the men selected in Acts 6, went far beyond that of a deacon. Philip was an evangelist (Acts 8:26; 21:8). Stephen, although never referred to as an evangelist, ministered as an evangelist (Acts 6:8–7:60). Their ministries are closer to those of an elder than of a deacon. Neither Acts 6 nor any other passages ever call those men deacons. God used those seven men to accommodate a specific need in the early church. Perhaps seven were selected because that was apparently the number of persons appointed to transact business publicly in Jewish towns.

III. THE ROSTER OF THOSE SELECTED (v. 5)

"The saying pleased the whole multitude; and they chose Stephen, a man full of faith and of the Holy Spirit, and Philip, and Prochorus, and Nicanor, and Timon, and Parmenas, and Nicolas, a proselyte of Antioch."

The apostles' suggestion united the two factions that had begun to form. God accomplished His purpose, and the devil's effort was thwarted. The church ended up being more unified than it was before. If the Grecians' complaint hadn't become known, the two groups might have stayed at odds with each other. But solving their grievances welded them together.

Luke says, "They chose." I believe the members of a church should select from among them men who are full of the Spirit, wise, and of honest report—men who can lead them. The Jerusalem church selected Stephen, Philip, and five others not mentioned again in Scripture: Prochorus, Nicanor, Timon, Parmenas, and Nicolas, who was a proselyte from Antioch. It is significant that all seven names are Greek names. The church unanimously chose seven Grecian Jews to lead them! That proves their love for unity. If the same situation arose today in our democratic society, we'd probably choose three Palestinians, three Grecians, and one Gentile proselyte, so all sides could have equal say. But the early church chose seven Grecians to lead them. What Satan tried to sow as discord grew to be wonderful unity. When the Hellenistic Jews saw the humility and concern of the Hebrews, their love and respect for them intensified. Because they were the majority, the Hebrews could have chosen whomever they wanted, but they voted in seven Grecian Israelites. Those seven men began to administrate the church, and the apostles returned to the Word.

IV. THE RESULTS OF SPIRITUAL ORGANIZATION (vv. 6-7)

"Whom they set before the apostles; and when they had prayed, they laid their hands on them. And the word of God increased, and the number of the disciples multiplied in Jerusalem greatly; and a great company of the priests were obedient to the faith."

After the congregation chose the seven, they presented them to the apostles to be commissioned. The laying on of the apostles' hands was simply an expression of the oneness of the whole church with them in their ministry. The leaders were ordained, and the church was organized. Because the apostles had more time and the members had renewed love for each other, "the word of God increased." When the Word increased, "the number of the disciples multiplied in Jerusalem greatly." And a shocking thing happened: many of the priests believed. The ordinary priests, who were looking for their Messiah, found Him in Jesus Christ. The church needs to accommodate what the Spirit of God is doing by providing enough structure to make it effective. That's what the church of Jerusalem did— and look at what happened!

Focusing on the Facts

1. Biblical church organization always _____ ministries that the Spirit has _____ _____ (see p. 60).
2. Does Acts 1-5 suggest that the Jerusalem church had already started to organize itself? Explain, supporting your explanation with Scripture (see p. 61).
3. What is the essence of organization (see p. 61)?

4. Describe the growth of the church in Jerusalem (see p. 62).
5. Explain the three tactics Satan used against the early church (see pp. 63-64).
6. Who are the "Hebrews" in Acts 6:1? Who are the "Grecians"? What was the attitude of the Hebrews toward the Grecians (see pp. 64-65)?
7. Explain the Jewish procedure for providing for the poor and the widows (see p. 65).
8. What is the significance of 1 Timothy 5:3-16 (see p. 65)?
9. What activities of the church can the phrase "serve tables" include (see p. 66)?
10. What are some arguments against having no organization within the church? Respond to them biblically (see p. 66).
11. According to Ephesians 4:11-12, church leaders should strive for what goal (see pp. 67-68)?
12. What were the priorities of the apostles (Acts 6:4; see p. 68)?
13. Explain the key words of 1 Timothy 4:13. What do those words define (see p. 69)?
14. What insight do 1 Corinthians 9:14 and Galatians 6:6 give into the preacher's commitment (see p. 70)?
15. List the basic requirements for church ministry (see pp. 70-71).
16. Were the men selected in Acts 6 deacons? Explain (see p. 72).
17. What is significant about the seven men the Jerusalem church chose (see p. 72)?
18. Describe the results of spiritual organization (Acts 6:6-7; see p. 73).

Pondering the Principles

1. The events of Acts 6 underscore the importance of meeting the needs of those who are unable to care for themselves. Some Christians, fearing being labeled as liberal or being accused of teaching a social gospel, have completely neglected this vital expression of our faith. Both the Old and New Testaments stress our obligation to use our resources to help others. Read 1 John 3:14-19, and then memorize verses 17-18. Begin this month to budget a certain amount of money that you can use to help others on a regular basis. Be alert to the needs of people in your church, family, school, workplace, and neighborhood.

2. The apostles knew their priorities: prayer and teaching the Word. Every church leader should share those same priorities. However, this responsibility doesn't stop with leaders—every believer should make the study of God's Word and prayer his priorities. How diligent and faithful are you at both? Have you allowed other responsibilities or activities to crowd out your personal time with the Lord? Have you neglected your relationship with Him? If so, take time now to ask God to forgive you for neglecting Him. Ask Him to revive your hunger and thirst to know Him and His Word. Decide on a time each day you can commune with Him through prayer and the study of His Word. Determine to be faithful to your decision, regardless of how you feel, and to make it a time of fellowship with the Lord—not a time of ritual. Starting today, read through Psalm 119 in a modern translation, meditating on it and praying it to God.

Scripture Index

Topical Index

Ananias and Sapphira, 10-14

Barclay, William, on Jewish assistance for widows, 65

Boldness, 36-38, 43, 57

Church
  boldness of early, 36-38, 43, 55-56
  caring nature of, 65, 75
  discipline, 12-16, 20
  divisions in early, 63-65
  evangelism of early, 8-11, 16-17, 24, 36, 39-45, 55-56
  framework of. *See* organization of
  growth of early, 8-10, 17, 62
  influence of early, 42-43, 45-57
  leadership of early, 70-73. *See also* Leadership
  meeting needs. *See* caring nature of
  membership, 14-17
  message of early, 31-32, 36-38
  mission of early. *See* evangelism of
  organization of early, 59-75. *See also* Organization
  persecution of early, 26-36, 55-56. *See also* Persecution
  persistence of early. *See* boldness of
  power of early, 17-19, 25, 38
  purity of early, 10-17, 25
  results of early. *See* influence of
  sin in early, 10-13
  unbelievers in, 14-16
  unity of early, 10, 72-73

widows and, 65
witness of early. *See* evangelism of
Commitment, spiritual. *See* Church, membership
Conviction
  characteristics of, 46-47
  goals of, 47-48
  illustration of, 45-46
  responses to, 57
    belief, 55-56
    hostility, 49-50
    indecision, 50-55

Deacons. *See* Leadership
Devotions, daily, 75

Elders. *See* Leadership
Evangelism
  boldness in. *See* Boldness
  responses to. *See* Conviction
  See also Church, evangelism of early

Flogging, Jewish procedure of, 55

Gamaliel, 50-55, 57
Gospel, responses to. *See* Conviction
Government
  obedience to, 34
  righteous disobedience to, 34-35

Healings. *See* Miracles
Holiness
  corporate. *See* Church, purity of early
  personal, 21

81

Holy Spirit, miraculous gifts of.
See Miracles

Influence, 42-43
Ironside, Harry, on church discipline, 13

Josephus
  on Judas of Galilee, 53
  on Sadducees's acquiescence, 51
Judas of Galilee, 52-53

Leadership, spiritual
  commissioning of, 73
  crisis of, 67
  delegation by, 66
  distinctions between, 72
  distractions of, 67
  origin of, 71
  priorities of, 66-70
  reputation of, 71
  requirements for, 70-73
  salary of, 69-70
  to be men, 70-71
  See also Organization
Lucifer. *See* Satan

McCheyne, Robert Murray, on a holy minister, 11
Ministers. *See* Leadership
Ministry. *See* Church
Miracles
  apostolic, 17-19, 25
  cessation of, 19
  dismissal of, 36
Missions. *See* Church, evangelism of early
Moody, Dwight L., great Chicago fire and, 55

Organization, spiritual
  balance regarding, 60, 66-67
  essence of, 61

need for, 60
reasons for, 61-70
results of, 73
specifics of, 61-62
virtue of, 60, 66
See also Leadership

Pastors. *See* Leadership
Persecution
  forms of, 26-27, 63
  governmental, 34-35
  inevitability of, 26-27, 39
  not for righteousness' sake, 39
  reasons for, 28-36, 39, 63
  response toward, 39, 55-56
  reward for, 27-28
  source of, 26, 63
  subtlety of, 26-27
Pharisees, description of, 28, 51
Preachers. *See* Leadership
Purity. *See* Holiness

Quiet Time. *See* Devotions

Sadducees, description of, 28-31, 51
Salvation. *See* Church, membership; Conviction
Satan
  authority of, 26
  fall of Lucifer, 26
  goal of, 26
  God's overruling of, 26, 30
  system of, 26
  titles of, 26
Scripture, accurately interpreting, 57
Service, Christian. *See* Church
Signs, 18-19. *See also* Miracles
Stripes. *See* Flogging

Talmud
  on procedure of flogging, 55

Moody Press, a ministry of the Moody Bible Institute, is designed for education, evangelization, and edification. If we may assist you in knowing more about Christ and the Christian life, please write us without obligation: Moody Press, c/o MLM, Chicago, Illinois 60610.